Dear Jay,

MW00527250

Thank you for sharing your journey through some very difficult times in your life. You have a talent for capturing and conveying profound life struggles in a few descriptive words.

I am a Psychiatric Mental Health Nurse and have worked in this area for over 40yrs. I am ANCC certified to work with Adults and Children and Adolescents.

Your book would be very helpful to use as a starting point for discussions related to addiction and depression. Many are not able to articulate their feeling of despair and do not recognize when or how to seek help. I endorse this book and hope it will be published as a tool to be used by others with similar issues.

Best regards,
Sharon Crouse ARNP

◆ ◆ ◆

I have been in the drug and alcohol rehabilitation field for 34 years and I think Mr. Richardson has written a very engaging book in which people, young, old, male or female, addicts or alcoholics or those who know them, will be able to relate! The first half of *A Bird's Journey* is an epic 107-page emotional roller coaster ride of a poem telling the story of his lifelong battles with drugs, alcohol, relationships, and journey toward recovery. Readers will also enjoy and benefit from the second half of the book with nearly 100 pages of poetry written throughout his life dealing with world issues, veteran's affairs, relationships, and drug/alcohol abuse and recovery. I look forward to having his book on my shelf and passing it on to those in recovery.

Sincerely,
Richard McLaughlin, Ph.D.
Licensed Psychologist
Orlando VA Medical Center

◆ ◆ ◆

I am a social work therapist who specializes in substance abuse treatment and have read Jay Richardson's, "A Bird's Journey" and was very impressed with the work and the passion of this journal book of poetry. I feel this work would benefit others and help with the identification of their journey through addiction and recovery.

I fully endorse this book and hope it will be published as a tool to be used by others in recovery.

Sincerely,
Kathleen E. Rashid

◆ ◆ ◆

Addicts walk a tightrope when they enter recovery. It is easy to fall off or choose to jump off. Hearing the stories of others who have emerged from the darkness of their illness into the light of a new life helps inspire recovering addicts to persevere and continue to navigate that tightrope. *A Bird's Journey* tells a harrowing tale of alcohol and drug addiction: the extreme risk taking and the heartbreaking consequences that inevitably follow. It is a reminder that using is like being on an elevator heading down—one can get off on any floor before arriving in the basement. In Bird's hopeful early recovery, finding love inspires him but also tests him. He fails the test and is shattered. Picking up the pieces he builds real and lasting recovery. *A Bird's Journey*, written in verse, evokes powerful imagery that conveys ecstasy, fear, sadness, anger and love. It is ultimately a story of hope and redemption that will inspire others in all stages of recovery.

Stuart Spangenberg, Licensed Clinical Social Worker, Certified Addictions Professional, Substance Abuse Professional, Certified Case Manager

To Rick Maxfield,
   I'll always have your back
brother!
      Love always,
            Bird

A "Bird's" Journey

by

Jay C. "Bird" Richardson

DORRANCE
PUBLISHING CO
EST. 1920
PITTSBURGH, PENNSYLVANIA 15238

Dorrance Publishing Co
585 Alpha Drive
Suite 103
Pittsburgh, PA 15238
Visit our website at www.dorrancebookstore.com

ISBN: 978-1-6480-4363-5
eISBN: 978-1-6480-4385-7

Contents

Part Two
Poems Written through the Years 1988-2010

Acknowledgments

I put my heart and soul into this book, but many other contributing factors were involved in order to make this come to life. Every person I've ever encountered has played a role in this tale, be it large or small. Many thanks are due.

First off I need to thank my higher power for keeping me around and seeing fit that a wretched soul like me can maybe give something back and possibly help or inspire others, who also walk a shadowy path, to stray into the light. I'm not one to sit and write usually. Poetry just happens for me. I truly look at it as a gift that was given.

Thanks to the multitude of AA and NA rooms and members around the world. Whenever times get tough there is always a place for us to go. If there's not, start one; it just takes two. It took me twenty years in and out of these rooms to hopefully get it, but just for today, I got it.

To my parents, John and Gayle Richardson, I could apologize the rest of my life and it would not be enough. I'm so sorry. Know that the paths I walked were my choices. You both were always there to provide a myriad of different routes. My higher power, however, saw fit for me to walk from the light into darkness and back out again. I would not be the man I am today, or will be tomorrow, if it were not for this arduous journey. Thank you for being there. Now rest easy and worry no longer. I can apologize no more for my past.

To my sisters: Jill, thanks for being the grounded one. Every family needs one. Dawn, it's not too often a family has two black sheep, but here we are. Throw in Uncle Vern and we're a little herd. Thank you for encouraging the arts, constantly broadening my spectrum on things and always believing that I could do it. You're both amazing women and a little brother could not be prouder.

My children, Kayla, Rhody, and Gage, I'm sorry my priorities got so distorted. I promise to spend the rest of my days making up for that lost time. I wrote this book in hopes that you'll read about my journey and not have to walk it yourself. The choices are always up to you.

Kim and Becca, thank you for showing me how to experience real emotions. Be it true love or true anguish, it was true.

To all those who watched me on my journey or joined me hand in hand:

My childhood friends: Ryan "Babe" Crouse, Yancy Unger, Jay Wimer, Chad Smith, Kent Bitting, my first girlfriend Kendra Mayers, and the Moore sisters, Susan, Robin, and Cindy. Cindy, you are very missed.

My teenage friends: the Dungeons and Dragons crew, Steve Boyle, Zac Varela, Chris Guimarin, Josh Gonzales, James Nance, and Jason Janski. My high school breakfast bong hits club, Robert "B" Becker, Jay Titterington, and Dan Nolan. The hooligans, Charlie and Ty Cortwright, Matt Scriven, Matt Huff, Anthony "BooBoo" Martin, Paul Beohm (you will be missed, big guy), Eiron Weibking, Suzan Lundberg Cortwright, Michelle "Schmell" Maxwell, and Dave Lombardo. The "real" wild started with you guys. Dave, I could write a whole book just about our many adventures together, and maybe one day I will.

To Thumper and the Screw Crew, what a summer I can't remember but will never forget.

To my Army buds, Dave Hulle, Deron Eunice, Bentley, Faust, Danny Burdiez, the military will never again be the same.

To Mandy Moore, Suzie Denoo, Amy Booth and Michelle Ricken. I was incapable of real love at the times you were in my life. I was selfish and I'm sorry. If I could have ever gotten on the same page, who knows? You're phenomenal, ladies. Thanks for having been a part of my life.

To Chris Mallicote, in and out of each other's lives so many times, I hope you found peace. I miss you.

To Jer, Josh, and Rick, organized crime never looked so good. How we're all still alive, I'll never know.

To my Ft. Collins friends, "Neighbor Dave" Rogers, Ethan Mead Teed, Jeemy Shelton, Holly Panetta, Shelly Brown Renner, Josh Nance, and Celestial Beam, great times were had. Here's to "Church" and Ft. Fun.

To Mrs. Caroline Hayes, for making me write my first poem. Look at what you inspired.

To Ben "Benny Boy" Christensen, you'll always be my little brother.

To Jonathan "Fish" Fisher, my getaway driver, you've always been a good friend. To Zach Lewis, for being there in the toughest of times. To Zac and Carrie Johns and their kids, what a great family. Thanks to all of you for being there when I was at the bottom.

To Scott Reed, for proofreading, Sutton Smith, for listening, and Kerry Filipsa, for her encouragement and enthusiasm.

To Uncle Vern just because.

To all those that have had to endure my poetry readings while I fine-tuned them. Thanks.

Last but not least, to all of those that I might have forgotten, do not think that you were forgotten intentionally. You should be surprised that I can remember anything with this pickled bean. Without the characters I've encountered in life, tales could not be told. Thanks to everyone.

Foreword

A "Bird's" Journey was started in my first venture into the psych ward in mid-July 2008. I had always wanted to do my life's story as a poem; however, it always seemed such a monumentally daunting task. But here, it looked like I was going to have some free time. I dove in feverishly, thinking the sooner it was complete, the sooner I could kill myself, leaving behind something of possible value. By the end of my fifteen-day stay, I was desperately trying to hold on to some reason to live and was only halfway complete with the story.

The poem was put on the "backburner,," as one week after my release, I was arrested for my third DUI and spent the next month in jail. Upon my release, I lasted another week or so "blind drunk" until the night I decided the story wasn't worth finishing. I found myself on the side of the street, eyeing busses and wondering if their oncoming speeds would be enough to get the job done.

Enter my second trip to the psych ward, whereas A "Bird's" Journey was revived and work began again in early September. The poem was completed in the first week of November in a VA drug, alcohol, and mental health facility.

Poetry from the past twenty-two years was then added on in part two. This was done in chronological order from age sixteen to thirty-eight. It can be read at your convenience or you'll find parenthesis at the end of chapters dictating which poems were written at that part of my life.

This compilation was first read by a counselor at the facility, after which he gathered other counselors to sit in and listen to the tale. It got a positive response from all and suggestions to publish were made.

With all that I've stolen, cheated, and taken in this life, hopefully with this I can give something back. Even if one person gains something from this endeavor, I've succeeded.

Take what you want, leave the rest.

Please enjoy A "Bird's" Journey.

Part One

A "Bird's" Journey

Chapter 1

The Farm Boy

A sheltered young boy
grew up on a farm
his parents made sure
he could come to no harm.

"Jaybird," they did call him
as a term to endear
and a fine young man
they intended to rear.

A small town of two thousand
in rural PA
came home hunting small game
after school every day.

At the age of nine
with a shotgun he was fine
at the age of thirteen
with a rifle he was keen
this would play a part
in his life unforeseen.

Established and knew
what he was going to be
his parents so thrilled
couldn't wait to see.

A star athlete
and
a straight-A student
into theater
well mannered
and with the girls so prudent.

Parents so happy
the young teenage boy too.
no one could see
what was about to ensue.

A job transfer for Dad
to Denver
a big city
the boy not wanting to go
filled with such self-pity.

"I know who I am.
I know who I'll be.
Leave me with Grandpa
just wait and you'll see."

But the pleas fell
on empty ears,

"We'll buy you an aquarium
to quell your fears."

but the boy felt cheated
and fell into tears.

Chapter 2

The City Boy

So to the big city
I did go
with all that pity
and anger in tow
they didn't see it now
but it soon would show.

Now the first day of school
I'm trying to act cool
but with overalls
and a briefcase
I looked quite the fool.

So I'm not the big fish
in a small lake anymore
and from now on
I don't even recognize the score.

I struggled to fit in
the nerds my new crew
for the farm boy now
everything was all new.

The anger now poured forth so free
the Amish country was no longer
my "cup of tea"
everyone just wait
and soon you'll all see.

Chapter 3

Cherry Creek, 90210

I get into high school
and my grades are not too bad
I occasionally miss home
I'm still a bit sad.

A school of four thousand
one of the wealthiest in the nation
after our football games in a stadium with Astroturf
is our celebration.

But then as fate will have it
I meet Kim
and fall in love
my high school sweetheart
my turtledove.

Can she ease the pain
this first true love
like a glorious angel
sent from above?

And soothe the pain
indeed she did
a love like this
had never existed.

And in all this
there was glorious joy
'til she broke my heart
with another boy.

But this was my true love
as any sixteen-year-old would know
so of course
I had to give it another go.

I kept coming back
for another beating
three times over
'til love was fleeting.

My true love
your beauty is your lure
but my heart and mind
can take it no more.

I put my emotions
up on a shelf
and just walk away
from my former self.

(See pages 72-78)

Chapter 4

Twilight

I run the opposite
of what I once was
no longer a geek
I'm a thug now, cuz'.

And now from the darkness
pent up inside
comes forth a steed
I aim to ride.

Straight to Hell
and never back.
What happened, Mom and Dad?
I was on the right track.

In high school now
I become the party king
and all the girls
are naught but a fling.

My childhood name
now shortened to "Bird"
I had no complaint
so I said not a word.

My last two years of school
I'm dealing drugs
my gentle nerds
now replaced with thugs.

An acid dealer
is now my claim to fame
and I'm so slick
I put the rest to shame.

An alcoholic by the time
I graduate school
drinking and drugs
are my Golden Rule.

I was voted most likely
not to see three-O
and if I have it my way
I'll make it so.

As for the heart?
Well, to keep sane
cold was all
that would now remain.

And that door sat shut
for eighteen years
when another woman broke through
and I once again could shed tears.

But that is still
later on in the story
before that I must get
to my drug-dealing glory.

(See pages 79-81)

Chapter 5

College

Once into college
I barely squeaked by
class was for losers
drug dealers were fly.

A dealer of acid, 'shrooms and pot
I didn't make it to class often
but I sure dealt a lot.

And my drinking tricks
had now evolved
beer bong a liter of vodka
and my troubles are solved.

The cops knew me by name,
                Honk, Honk,
            "Hey there, 'Bird'!"
As I walked down the street
arrested seven times
my first semester was complete.

Chapter 6

Jail "Bird" Makes a Deal

I decided that court
was not for me,

> "Catch me if you can, coppers,
> I'll wait and see."

It didn't take long
and I was no longer free.

Now my father,
being an influential man, said,

> "Listen here, Judge,
> I think I have a plan.
> Turn my son over
> there's a recruiter across the street
> they'll straighten him out
> with combat boots on his feet!"

So out of my cell
I immediately did walk
across to the Armed Forces
to have a little talk.

> "Let's see what your test scores
> say about you, young man.
> My goodness, hooah,
> a ninety-nine on the exam."

"In the Air Force
we need missiles that fly,
a nuclear physicist in the Navy,
just don't ask why,
or in the Army
you can shoot guns
and maybe die."

"There you go, recruiter,
that last one I'll try."

"So if I sign up
when would I ship out?
A one-year delayed-entry program,
go on,
get out.

And with my test scores
where do you think I could go?"

The recruiter says,

"Son, you pick it
and we'll make it so."

Well, aloha to me
the infantry I'll be
and the Hawaiian Islands
I'd love to go see.

"Judge, I went and signed the paper,
you'll have a year to solve this caper.
And if for me
you try to reach
you'll have to find me
in Cocoa Beach."

But before I escape
my parents see to it
a thirty-day drug and alcohol program,

"You'll like it and do it!"

So I give all the answers
that they want to hear
finish thirty days perfectly
while drinking a beer.

Chapter 7

"Spike" and the Screw Crew

Now off to the beach
I did run
play some volleyball
catch some sun
deal some drugs
and have some fun.

First day I show up
to check out the scene
many small groups hanging out
if you know what I mean.

By the end of the week
I had brought 'em all together
and the Screw Crew was born
with "Spike" as their tether.

A girl named me such
because of my hair
bleach blond and spiky
and without a care.

And I named them so
because it was true
getting screwed
or screwed up
was all we would do.

So every day
a few more would arrive
I'd give them their beach names
and show them how to survive.

I had Thumper and Taz
Spike Junior and Doc
just to name a few
'cause they came 'round the clock.

And we'd watch the sun set
and we'd sit in the sand
build a bonfire
and hold a girl's hand
sing Kumbaya
with a beat-up guitar
make love on the beach
and then look at a star
in retrospect
some of my best times by far.

And before I knew it
my year was through
and I had to say goodbye
to "Spike"
and the Screw Crew
and to all my beach friends
I bid thee farewell
and adieu.

Chapter 8

In the Army Now

Now off to the Army
it was time to go
my bleach-blond hair
and suntan aglow.

First day in the barracks
 I threw down my ruck
the black guy next to me said,

> "Who in the fuck?"

The brother next to him said,

> "I see what you mean,
> this dude's right out of
> the Hollywood scene."

And so from day one
I was "Hollywood"
sometimes a name fits
just fits as it should
and from then on out
"Hollywood" stood.

And as we all know
this military overseas tour
was to be my cure
from alcohol
fighting
and looking to score.
Take away these defects
and you'll want them
no more.

But much to my surprise
and utter dismay
it looked like alcohol
and drug abuse
were here to stay
a partier's wet dream
I would have to say
and the Army needed me
in a whole different way
and the drug dealer inside
was ready to play.

Under investigation
at one point of my career
dealing acid and ecstasy
and living without fear.

But even with Leavenworth
as a threat
I'm not done dealing
oh, no
not yet.

For me, the adrenaline rush was intense
and it made my heart beat quick.
Man, this is a blast
and I really don't give a frick.

I need this now
that immediate surge
and another addiction
begins to emerge.

Now don't get me wrong
in the field I was good
everything exact
and just as it should.

A warrior now trained
with the skill to kill
I was so good
I could do it at will.

I could pass through the jungle
simply unabated
but once back in the real world
I was always drug and alcohol faded.

I was doing drugs
I never thought I'd do
shooting up heroin and smoking ice
to me was all new.

(See pages 82-90)

Chapter 9

Rehab Round Two

So ice was now my favorite hit
and the Army now thought
an outpatient drug and alcohol program
would be a nice fit.

I tried to skate through
once again
but a three-month inpatient program
would be the end.

But before I can enter
and get my life right
I fail a piss test
I guess maybe
I'm not too bright.

And so three years
had flown on by
and the end of "Hollywood"
came to a close
an experience left
with minimal morose.

Chapter 10

Gangsta "Bird"

I finished my tour
with my infantry skill
spit shine a boot
with my hands I can kill
polish a hell of a floor
or your head with lead I can fill
and if none of that works
I can always sell you a pill.

I find myself in Ft. Collins, Colorado
and I think I'm in a dream
this place just can't be as cool
as it may seem.

College girls and parties abound
a little slice of heaven
I think I've found.

Now what to do
with all that I've militarily mastered
well-organized crime came calling
looking for a drug-dealing ex-military bastard
and don't you believe it
I aimed to achieve it.

And like a phoenix
"Bird" reemerged
what scant feelings left
had now been purged.

Within six months
I'm the left-hand man
and with that comes
a different plan.

You see now
I'm on a different scale
in the drug dealer's fish pond
I'm now a whale.

Moving now
many pounds at a time
it makes me nervous
even to finish this rhyme.

And the Mexican mafia
was a slight bit shake'n
at the business we took
and the money we were make'n.

And then one day
the opposition stood in my way
and my paid gorillas
had something to say.

A Mexican Mafioso
was slammed to the street
unfortunate for him
headfirst on concrete.

And so a hit
was put out on me
and most people said,

        "Bird, it's now time to flee!"

        "No," I said,
        "I think I'll lay low."
        My Boss said, "Do it quick
        and just make it so."

The next two months
I went underground
dropped out of sight
and made not a sound.

Until one night
an afterhours club called my name
and to be quite honest
I was missing my fame.

So I went to "The Loft"
thought I'd have a drink
and hear a tune
didn't think it necessary
to bring along a goon.

Sat at the bar
having a shot
a tap on the shoulder
and I'm put on the spot.

Now who would interrupt
my drinking affair
but a Mexican Mafioso Générale
and his men standing there.

"Sit," I said,
"Let's do a shot."
"I'm not going anywhere.
It seems you have me caught."

A dozen shots later
and I have no more cares
a pushing match with the Générale
finds him on the wrong end
of a three-story
flight of stairs.

The trip to the bottom
left a broken man
neck, legs, and arms obviously
and the rest was up to CAT scan.

For the rest of his days
he walked with a cane
a shell of a man
with constant pain.

And as a whale
it was time to swim
to stay in this pond
my future looked dim.

(See pages 91-94)

Chapter 11

Cheyenne

I don't want you to think
that dealing was all that I knew.
I managed pet stores
and worked with bands, too
and to my blackout drinking games
nightly I was true.
Six years this was my cover
and a good one at that, too
but it was time
to take a real job transfer
and in Wyoming I was due.

To fix a failing pet store
was now the job at hand
don't know if you've ever been to Cheyenne
it truly is a Godforsaken land.

Stayed hidden and drunk
for six months straight
then rumor had it I was found
and again
it was time to deliberate.

Chapter 12

Virginia Beach

Just as luck would have it
my Navy sister in Virginia Beach
had given me a call.

"I'm shipping out and occasionally
need someone to watch my condo, truck, and all."

I need to stay one step ahead
or certainly I'll just wind up dead.

"I'm on my way, sis,"
is all I said.

I try to leave
the drug world behind
on the East Coast
I should be hard to find.

I acquire another job
at a local pet store
I'm still drinking a good bit
and then I drink some more.

Then the phone rings one day
and it's my ex-Boss.

"The heat is on.
I'm at a loss.

I need to leave,
at all costs."

"Come on out, Boss,
I don't know
what my sister will say,
but I'm sure she'll be okay
with a short little stay."

So now the biz
had come to me
but we both decide to try
to stay drug dealer free.

We'd start over here
the potential was rife
find real jobs
and live without strife.
heck, my Boss had even brought
a possible wife.

But before we could move out
and find our own place to dwell
the potential new wife
had a surprise to tell.
In a few months
her stomach would begin to swell
and she'd rather be back
in Colorado as well.
And so to my ex-Boss and best friend
I said, "Farewell."

Chapter 13

Merritt Island, Florida

I still decided
that I would try and settle down.
I moved to Merritt Island, Florida,
where a small condo was found.

Picked up a job
managing another pet store.
Lived the mundane life
strewn with the everyday bore
but it was much better
than the death sentence tour.

This lasted a month
and one night I was drinking extra heavy
and had to change lanes
around a fifty-seven Chevy.

I guess this is where
I should have used my blinker
but with fifteen shots of Jager in me
I'm not much of a thinker.

First thing that I saw
was a red-and-blue flashing light.

> "Those can't be for me!"
> I said with a fright.

The next thing that I know
a white light is in my eye.

"Son, are you able to step over here
And spell 'DUI'?"

Six months
I lose my license
nine months
I'm on probation.
six months
I get my license back
time to celebrate
with a libation.
Oops
this second DUI
is going to be
a costly litigation
and damn
I still have three months
left on probation.
Sorry, Mom and Dad,
a fully furnished condo's yours
it's time for another
"Bird" migration.

I sell my Jeep
the following day
to have some cash
to be on my way
power of attorney letter
is written to say,

"Do what you will with everything, Mom and Dad,
I'm gone today."

Get to the airport
to head for an isle.
Bahamas might be nice
to hang for a while.

Traveling with two Army duffle bags
and a dog named George
my mentally retarded midget canine
with whom the best of friendships
was forged.

Chapter 14

George

Let me step back
and tell you the tale
of a pituitarian dwarf
and hydrocephalic dog for sale
and a vet check
that he would quickly fail.

The cutest of pups
and for a Jack Russell serene
half head and half body
but missing something blatantly
on the chromosomal scene.

Sold to a family
in Virginia Beach
returned as defective
and a reimbursement of their money
they soon would beseech.

I was given instructions
to put the Jack down

"I can't do that, Doc,"
I said with a frown.

"How long, Vet,
do you think he'll live?"

"Two years and no more,
I think I'd give.
Seizures of the brain
will be his demise."

"Well then, I'll keep him and love him
till the day he dies."

So the decision was made
to take the little guy home
and around my sister's condo
he proceeded to roam.

A squeaky hamburger
was his favorite first game
but now it was time
to find him a name.

Flipping the channels
on that same day
and Cartoon Network
came my way.

An old Bugs Bunny cartoon
is what I saw
and a big, hairy yeti
had him in his paw.

The yeti pounds him on the head
and he did say,

"I will name him George,
And I will hug him
and pet him
and squeeze him."

and George
was here to stay.

George traveled everywhere with me
in a backpack
and a shortage of friends
he did not lack.

A legend he became
in every club and bar.
East Coast
West Coast
a frick'n rock star.

And every establishment
that came our way
it was not my name
that they would say,

it was "George is here!
Hip, hip, hooray!"

Chapter 15

Denver Again

Now to get back
to the story at hand
dreaming of islands
and deserted beach sand.

So I'm at the airport
and I'm ready to fly
these planes can get up there
but I always fly really high.

The guy at the counter
is talking three months' quarantine.

"He's just a small dog,
I don't know what you mean!"

Laws are laws
and the islands are out
the situation now
is an immediate reroute.

First turn that I take
is into an airport bar
a sour realization
that I'm not going far
a dozen stiff drinks
and I'm again a drug czar.

Colorado is easy
and already known.
I buy a ticket
and to there we're flown.

One of my best friends, James,
who's wheelchair bound,
has a house in Denver
that's safe and sound.

For a better chum in life
a person could not ask.
Straightening out my evil ways
is now the uphill task.

Five grand in my pocket
and I think I'll start a small biz
or I could drink and drug it all away
says the inside junky wiz.

Two weeks to the day
and the money's all gone
wanting a cocktail to figure out
how things went wrong.
I'm starting to see
that it's me all along.

Chapter 16

Cancun, Mexico

Now what to do
with no money or job
well, I find a friend in Cancun
to help continue my ruin.

He has a company
called the "Party Cruise."
The boat barely stays afloat
with this much booze.

Now George and I have it good
the way that party animals should
living in the Mexican hood
like American kings would.

Every day we sleep in
get up and scour the beach
finding the hottest girls and coolest guys
and to them a wild party we preach.

We sell tickets
from noon to four
and at eight o'clock
we begin our drunken tour.

Our duty on the ship
is to show them how to have a good time.
If we're breaking the law
debauchery is our crime.

The women were fine
the drugs were cheap.
A fifth of tequila a night
would put me to sleep.

But after a six-month stay
visa's up
and it's time to be on my way.
So it's back to Denver
without a dime
as all my money
went to fiesta time.

Chapter 17

Denver Gets Dark

James tolerates
a year or so drunk
'til both he and I can see
I've turned out to be a punk.

He's decided he can no longer endure
the alcohol
late nights
and looking to score

"Sorry, 'Bird,'"
but I can take it no more."

Finding a new place
is now my chore.

I call my drinking
and drug buddy Rick.
Rick
let me tell you
is oh so slick.
Don Juan debonair
Johnny Depp is his look
and he can play all the women
right by the book.

So Rick and I
get a place to share
both working at a restaurant
without a care
and vodka and cocaine
were our favorite fare.

I dive deep
a fifth a day
the cocaine was there
to extend my stay.
I drank before work
to get me to go
then the bartenders there
would help keep up the show.

I drank all this liquor
because that I could.
I drank more
than an elephant should.

Chapter 18

Milo

Then one night
at a party downtown
the people had all left
and I said with a frown,

> "I wonder where my little buddy
> George could be?"

A search of the place
but George
I did not see.

Next day I started calling
those that were at the party
I hit them up
with a question sortie.

> "Have you seen him?"
> "Where could he be?"

But George's disappearance
no one did see.

I searched the concrete jungle
high and low
and time was now
my biggest foe.

I put up flyers
and called the pound
here's my number
call me if he's found.

But George was gone
my little best friend.
I entered a dark place
and a fifth and a half a day I would tend.

I sat in the dark
and drank on the couch.
To this sickened sorrow
all my friends can vouch.

Fifteen days
in a drunken stupor
I gotta give my liver credit
it was a real trooper.

Friends finally
drag me out to play
and it's to downtown again
I find my way.

We enter a bar
and the 'tender does say,

> "Where is George
> this fine drinking day?"

"Lost," I say,
"for over a fortnight
and at the end of this tunnel
I see not a light."

"Hang on!" the server says.
"Say it ain't so!
I think I saw George
a week ago
in the park
with the homeless
a small dog in tow.
I thought it was George
but knew the answer
had to be no."

Straight to the park
I do arrive
find some transients
a group of five,

"Does a little white dog
Yet survive?"

"Oh, Milo, I think
is of whom this man speaks.
He's been living with us
for a few weeks."

I take a few moments
and begin to talk.

"This Milo, where is he?"
"Oh, he's out for a walk."

I wait for a while
in hopes for my dog
but I'm starting to sober up
and I so do like my fog.

"Here's the address
of where I'll stay.
I'll throw beer and drugs
and money your way.
You bring me Milo
and I'll make your day!"

Three hours later
and three homeless at the door
with Milo in hand
I'll look for George no more.

Chapter 19

Out of Darkness

Now you would think
my drinking binge
could come now to an end
with the return
of my little buddy
and my best friend.

But for some reason
there's no end in sight
no idea of quitting
I don't even put up a fight.

And my deep, dark place
now won't allow me to work
I guess it's just another
drinking quirk.

I decide to get drunk
to make things better
if this isn't insanity
spelled right to the letter.

On December twenty-first
two thousand the year
I'm a total wreck
and if I have a soul is unclear.

For the first time ever
I wake up and feel
drinking
and drugs
have lost their appeal.

I can't take credit
for this lack of desire
a higher power
had to have quenched this fire.

I never thought
I'd ever quit
I mean, God damn,
I loved this shit.

But here it was
my final last call
and at the end of the tunnel
a light I saw.

Chapter 20

Light

I drop the bottle
and don't look back
check myself into jail in Florida
to start out anew
and get on the right track.

I do some time
go to church and AA
and every night I kneel down
give thanks and pray.

The day soon comes
and I get my release
a retired drug runner
now seeking only peace.

For three and a half months
I check myself into a recovery house
and in AA and sobriety
my soul I now souse.

(See pages 95-101)

Chapter 21

The One

One day I get a call
from my former Boss,

> "I'm getting married
> and a best man I need."

> "I'd love to be him," I said,
> "an honor, indeed."

To leave the halfway house
I cannot come back
but strength in my sobriety
I do not lack
and so to Florida I say,

> "I'll be right back."

I fly to Colorado
for the marriage so grand
my first big test
to make a sober stand
and my quest to live clean
my ex-Boss can understand.

A broken-down car
and a driving plight
my ex-Boss says,

"My sister will pick us up tonight
she'll be taking us to
the wedding site."

A short time later
and an angel walks in
tall and gorgeous
and built for sin.

She leaves really quick
to go get some gas
and to my ex-Boss
I have to ask,

"How is this
with all the time we spent
I've never met your sister
who's heaven sent?"

He looks me in the eye and says,
"This was no accident."

Becca was her name
and a lost moment by her side
would have been a shame.
Right out of the gate
love was the game.

I flew back down
to the Sunshine State
and every night on the phone
we'd talk real late.

A month and a half later
I flew back out
spent five more days
and now I had no doubt.

Becca has a lovely daughter
who's oh so sweet
and to be her father
would be a treat.

Forty-five days later
they came to see me
along with the beaches
and gators
and swaying palm tree
but I had one more surprise
for them to see.

"We'll look at some houses
your first day here
to try and get money
from your daddy dear."

So now the stage was set
for I had bought the house two weeks prior
for this girl I'd met
and we'd go to check it out
for the biggest surprise yet.

"So what would you think
of a house like this?"

"Why, this would be
a slice of bliss."

"I'll let you know
the price is right,"
and down on one knee
I make it my proposal sight.

The answer is "yes"
and I'm filled with glee
this woman will spend
the rest of her life
with me.

Two months later
and the marriage is set in stone
for all of eternity
I won't be alone.

(See pages 102-105)

Chapter 22

Life in Suburbia

An instant dad
of a young girl eight
to be a good father
I wish as my fate
but a secondhand dad
is all that I rate.

I try real hard
to get it right
but a strict background and a lack of knowledge
is my plight
and getting her to do what I want
is a constant fight.

And this woman
I courted for all of one hundred and twenty days
for some reason
doesn't always agree with my ways.

Eight months along
of ups and downs
this roller-coaster ride
knows no bounds.

And at this point
I quit going to AA
because there doesn't seem to be
enough time in the day.

And now's the moment
we get the news
her getting sick in the morning
was part of the clues.

We find out a baby
is on the way
hopefully
to save the day
but God surely knows
this is not the way.

My son is born
and a blessing it could be
will this save our marriage?
We'll just wait and see.

Six months later
and another Godsend
two babies now
we'll have to tend
and nine months later
another son is born
to protect my children
forever now I'm sworn.

Daycare is expensive
and times are tight
this monetary battle
is an uphill fight.

I'm basically working
just to pay for daycare
a stay-at-home dad I could be
I quickly become aware.

For the next two years
I stay home with the boys
raise 'em up right
and reap the joys.

I work at night
and weekends, too
getting up in the morning
was difficult to do.

But we make it work
my wife and I
two sailing ships in the night
just passing by.

After a couple of years
it's now become clear
the boys are old enough
for daycare without fear.

An opportunity to run an automotive company
soon comes my way
and this now becomes
my everyday.

The drug dealer
party life
now seems long ago.
I now live in suburbia
work
pull weeds
and mow.

The perfect home
the trophy wife
two-point-five kids
and a happy life.

Or so I think
it seems to be
but underneath there's something
I do not see.

Four and a half years
without a drink
I got this thing licked
or so I think.

Chapter 23

Enabled, but I Know Better

In two thousand five
the wife and I plan a getaway
with our best friends to Miami
for a short little stay.

Just prior to leaving
my wife does say,

> "Don't you ever want to cut loose
> and have a drink?"

> "I hadn't really thought about it," I think.

> "Well, maybe on a special occasion
> you could tip a few."

Well, with four and a half years sober
I guess I'm due.

Now after our trip
every day's a special day
and I drink every drink
that comes my way.

At home we split
a bottle of wine every night
and at most parties
I'm a drunken sight.

After two years drinking
the wife's had enough
she asks me to quit
which shouldn't be
too tough.

I put it down
and I'm okay with it
if it's my marriage
or drinking
I'll quit the shit.

For four months straight
I do not imbibe
maybe for the wrong reasons
'cause it's for my bride.

Her Christmas work party
and we get dressed up
an hour into it
with water in my cup.

Now around her friends
I don't have much to say
and my wife can get down
in a wild way.

She comes up to me and says,

> "Loosen up.
> If you want to pour out that water
> I'll let you refill your cup."

Before I can think
a Long Island I drink
and the party is on
just like you'd think.

Now it's not her fault
as I now know
I should have said,

                              "No thanks,
                              I don't think so."

But my addiction is strong
and my mind is weak
any chink in my armor
like an arrow it'll seek.

But our life goes on
I feel everything's fine
and we settle back in
to our nightly wine.

Chapter 24

The Cocaine Demon

In two thousand seven
I get a call
from an old friend
with whom I played volleyball.

"I have a politician friend
who's looking for blow.
I don't have any connections
you're the only one
I might know."

"Do you think you can help them out
on this one-time deal?
They don't know the cost or weight
so it may seem surreal."

"For an old friend like you,
not a problem," I say.
"I'll make seventy-five bucks
and a free eight ball today!"

Now no longer a dealer
what do I do with the free coke?
Well, the wife and I can do it
and that's no joke.

And what was to be
a one-time thing
we can now count on the phone
every other day to ring
and to a new addiction
we both now cling.

This goes on
for a nine-month blight
I've dropped forty pounds
and look an awful fright
and the worst part is
there's no end in sight.

And where I've had many demons
my wife had shown none
for all that was out there
cocaine was the one.

We go for days at a time
with no food or sleep
into the bedroom
when the kids aren't looking
we'd creep.
Papers on my desk
at work
are a heap
and cocaine
now into my soul
does seep.

We try to quit
and tell the politician,

            "Please, no more."

But the phone keeps ringing
and for coke
there's no cure.

We could even justify doing it
because the conversations were great.
We'd talk all night,
was it real early
or late?

Oh, who cares.
Take another hit.
Let's talk some more bullshit.
And if we ever run out
there's more we can get.

We'd smoke all night
'til the sun would rise
but after nine months straight
I saw tears in her eyes.

Towards the end
the politician's coke
was not enough.
We were now spending
our own money
to get the stuff.

Chapter 25

A Door Reopens

At the same time
we'd been doing marriage counseling
for the past half a year
and now the counselor said,

"I think you're in the clear.
Go on, kids,
enjoy life
love each other
and get out of here!"

A funny thing happened
inside me at this point.
That emotional door
that had long been closed
slowly would reopen
and long-dead emotions re-rose.

They came forth
slowly at first
and then quickly breached the dam
and I realized for certain
what a fool I am.

Like a blind man seeing
I opened my eyes
and right there before me
was the ultimate prize.

"What have I done
to deserve Becca?"

I immediately realize.

I rededicate myself to her
as these new feelings of real love
begin to stir.

For the next six weeks
I lived in bliss
adoration in my eyes
always looking to steal a kiss.

But the Cocaine Demon
still in our house did dwell.
I guess it was bliss
tainted with a whole bunch of Hell.

And then she revealed
that which I didn't see.

"Jay, I no longer love you,
It can no longer be,
I'm going to file
for a divorce decree."

My soul was shattered.
My heart ripped apart.

"We've got two little boys," I pleaded.
"Give me a fresh new start."

But the damage was done
and all these emotions I felt
mattered no longer
for in a cold place
she now dwelt.

(See pages 106-114)

Chapter 26

Spiral to the Bottom

My downward spiral
came fast
and hard
and sucking down liquor
just made it quicker.

I moved out of my house
to aimlessly wander
to look at my wife
and she not love me anymore
was too much to ponder.

I'm losing myself
I'm missing my wife
I've lost my house
my children
and my former life.

I existed in a blackout
most of the time now.
Still managing to get to work
but usually I don't know how.

Then one day
I got my pistol
and called my wife.

"I can take it no more!
I'm going to take my life!"

But before I pulled the trigger
or chambered a round
God guides me to the highway
and a hospital is found.

I end up in a VA Psych ward
and I'm losing my mind,

> "Can't somebody hear me?
> My mind I can't find!"

Maybe here
I can sober up
and truly unwind.

I spend fifteen days
to get my head straight.

> "Please don't release me now
> or death may be my fate!"

But they send me out
back into the fire
my drinking is heavy
my needs are dire.

One week to the day
I get my third DUI.
I have nothing to live for
and just want to die.

I end up going to jail
my heart and soul wail
I plead to the judge
but to no avail.

They eventually set me free
but depression now clouds
everything that I see.

I've lost my license to drive
most of my purpose to survive
and now I have no car
so in my sickness
I walk to the closest bar.

And all those feelings
long dormant
that upon me were thrust
just hurt so badly
it all seems unjust.

The darkest place I now walk
with no one to talk
will I jump off the cliff
or will I hesitate and balk?

The liquor takes hold
and makes the evil thoughts bold.
I think now maybe
my soul's been sold.

I can take it
no more.
I hate my life.
Oh, dear God,
I miss my kids
and wife.

I find myself standing
on the side of a street
in hopes the Devil
I'll soon meet.

Insanity
Insanity
I just want to be free
of drinking insanity.

The bus comes fast
the pain is too vast...

(See pages 115-119)

Chapter 27

Saved Again

But another divinely intervention takes place
and for some reason
I step back and walk
the demons are still there
my soul they still stalk.

I pick up the phone,

"Mom and Dad, I'm alone,
I don't want to live,"

I pitifully moan.

Back in the psych ward
I find myself again
thank God for the VA
and the sorrows they tend.

The assignment right now
is to find a reason to live
it'll have to be my children
and the unconditional love that they give.

In my sick mind
the problem at hand
is my wife
finding a new man.

To her
three months alone
is a long time
and my boys so young
a new daddy
she could prime.
My weakened mind
has an uphill climb.

After another five-day death delay
they send me on my way
if it was up to me
I'd be here to stay.

I make arrangements
for my fourth drug and alcohol program
maybe if I quit drinking and drugs
I'll find out
who I really am.

I have two weeks before I go in.
I stay with my parents
'cause they know
where I've been.

I arrive at their home
to find my job is gone
my wife has a restraining order
and my kids are a pawn.

(See pages 1120-129)

Chapter 28

Tools of Salvation

In a matter of three months
my whole life has dissolved
I enter the program
with much to be solved.

I think we all know the answer
drugs and alcohol's
my cancer.

I got twelve weeks
to figure it out
and the rest of my life
to fight this bout.

I delve deep
and look inside
on many a day
I was humbled and cried.

It scares me to look
at this life that I've led
and the various ways
that I should have been dead.

I'm finding my way
out through the haze.
my mind's getting clearer
and I'm having better days.

I still think about her
and wonder what she's doing
but I've learned to deal
with the feelings that are brewing.

Letting go is the hardest part
pain knows no bounds
when it comes to the heart.

But to keep my sobriety
and what's left of my sanity
I've got to let her be free
letting go is the most painful key.

Time is healing
what I could not
from whence I came
let it not be forgot.

I have a new set of tools
with which I can use
and drugs and alcohol
hopefully
I'll never again abuse.
it's the start of a new life
in which I can choose
and if I do this right
I know I can't lose.

And so out of my life's convolution
there's evolution
to hopefully
the ultimate solution.

And even a sick soul
as twisted as me
has another chance
as you can see.

The sun now rises
in a whole new light.
I still have gray days
but most are now bright.
Either way I'll march on
and fight the good fight.

I still go to AA or NA
and walk Twelve Steps every day.
It's a much easier path
I would have to say
but now I think
I should be on my way.

So now what for me
does the future hold?
Well, that would be presumptuous
and much too bold
and apparently, I hadn't listened
to my own story told.

I'd like to thank you
for reading my life in rhyme
so now go out and live,

"One day at a time."

(See pages 130-137)

Part Two

Poems Written through the Years
1988 to 2010

Prelude to The Little Girl Knows

The Little Girl Knows was written in 1988, my sophomore year of high school. It was the first poem I'd ever written. An assignment for a Creative Writing class taught by Mrs. Caroline Hayes at Cherry Creek High School. Upon grading Mrs. Hayes had me write the poem on the chalkboard for the rest of the class to read. Its outstanding reception opened the door to a poetic future.

I've written poems throughout the years and a multitude have been discarded. However, The Little Girl Knows has lasted twenty plus years and has turned out to be an always current piece.

The Little Girl Knows

Little girl, little girl
what was it you said
about the sun blotting out
and your world being dead?

You should have spoken sooner
when politicians were near
but they never came here
did they, my dear?

Now our Earth lies broken
where the bombs fell hard
hideously
horribly
scarred.

The politicians lie
far below
in their ballrooms of cement
their parties go on
like nothing new
yes, they are content.

You struggle for
your last few breaths
and soon join your relatives
in their deaths.

A push of a button
technology flies
is this our future
where everyone dies?

Prelude to Turning Love's Pages
and Melting Stone

Both of these poems were written to Kim during the tumultuous relation-ship of our "on again, off again" romance. Melting Stone won the Editor's Choice Award in 2003 from the National Poetry Society.

Turning Love's Pages

Oh, I was young
and she was younger
and neither knew
which way the world spun.
But all I know
is that as time passed
her heart was to be won.

And I the victor
strode a young gallant man
for I knew in my heart
that there was love in this plan.

And we all know
that first true love
and how we float upon the sky
never caring
whether
which
what
how
or why.

For all our focus
is upon that one
and Lord, she was so fine
and nothing else seemed to matter
except ensuring that she was mine.

And believe me
I was there
oh, day in and day out
always within an arm's reach
or at least a quiet shout.

Then the dreadful day
came crashing down
and I looked and looked
and pondered around
but my true love
was nowhere to be found.

So I took a seat
with my singed heart
and began to recollect
from the start.

I counted the ways
of how and why
and with each new reason
I thought I'd die.

But I was young
and she was younger
and perhaps I didn't know
that what she really needed
was a little time to grow.

Now I'm still young
she's not much younger
the years have added age
perhaps it's time
we reopen the book
and write another page.

Melting Stone

I don't know
it doesn't seem fair
I gave so much
with nothing returned
how funny love is
when love is yearned.

Bruised and battered
I stand alone
shall my heart soften
or remain stone.

My friends stick by me
they're always there
they all know
love just isn't fair.

Prelude to Soul Searching

Soul Searching was written around the period of graduation from high school. It was a time when love had been lost and being a romantic at heart, the pain was almost too much to bear. I was just learning the ins and outs of the underbelly of the city and was confused as to who I was then and who the future me was going to be.

Soul Searching

Out-of-place soul
drifting around
drift a bit farther
maybe you'll be found.

People speeding
'round and 'round
keep on going
'cause you won't be found.

Revered holy man
seeking only peace
we want to know
what's your release?

Con artist
fools
government press
only tell you what they want
the rest you guess.

Man of nature
displaced soul
tell me now
what is your goal?

City of vermin
reeking of trash
some you keep
the rest you smash.

Broken man
sight for sore eyes
tell them your stories
tell them your lies.

I've heard for most
all the tales around
oh, poor lost soul
will you ever be found?

Drug addict beast
bloated drunk
heed me now
before you're sunk.

When we were born
God set before us a goal
these are my last words
on finding your soul.

Prelude to The Trouble Is...

The Trouble Is... was written in basic training to Kim. A lonely period for any man, we were still trying to make things work. Drugs and alcohol had become a staple prior to enlisting and the Jay she loved was unfortunately never to be recovered.

The Trouble Is…

The trouble is…

While we were together
I was blind.

Now every day
I'm tortured to the soul.

You visit me in your own little ways
a sweet scent
a song of memories
something that you used to say
you visit me
many times a day.

The trouble is…

I got lost
but in the process
I paid the cost.
The greatest price of all, some say
the question the angels ask on judgment day.

"Did you ever share yourself and love another?"

"No," I scream. "No, never!"

But I know this is a meaningless endeavor
I loved but once
and not again, ever.

"How is this," the judges cry,
"you've come so far
on the day you die?"

When we lost touch
I lost my soul
and with that
you took my greatest goal.

To spend my life
with my heart's desire
to say anything else
I'd be a liar.

I miss our walks and talks
our hugs and kisses
holding hands and dreaming of distant lands
I miss sitting around and chatting life
I miss asking you to be my wife.

The trouble is...

I still love you.

Prelude to Would You Wipe Your Ass with a Dollar?

This was written after traveling to Korea, Japan, Taiwan, and Malaysia. Having spent time in these countries, it put a real perspective on just how good we have it in the United States. We are truly a sheltered culture that has created its own utopia.

Would You Wipe Your Ass with a Dollar?

Cold, hard green
can make a man mean
make you cheat a friend
or bluff family in the end.

Cold, hard green
can make a man sly
throws a glint in your eye
would you let somebody die
for a piece of money pie?

Cold, hard green
can make somebody think
about arsenic in your drink
for when you're cold in the ground
the insurance policy will be found
and your darling, sweet husband or wife
sits on the beach
the rest of their life.

Now ain't it a shame
that money's to blame
and only cold, hard green
can give you a name.

In some cultures
people trade for a living
they're a little more giving
a little more personal
and a little less greedy.

And they would wipe their asses
with our cold, hard greens
'cause basically
they don't know what it means.

Prelude to Army Green

Written in 1991 during the Persian Gulf War, I was assigned to the 25th Infantry stationed out of Oahu, Hawaii. This was a questioning time for any young person to have to face the horrors of war.

Army Green

Here I am in Army Green
acting big, bad, and mean
but inside I'm still the same
to me this all is just a game.

This is the game of life
a deadly game
of take or lose your life.

All because of a grenade toss
fragments fly at life's cost

"Grenade!!!" was all you had time to scream

and then in a flash
your life's naught but a dream.

And here I am in Army Green
acting big, bad, and mean
but inside I'm still the same
to me this all is just a game.

All because of the pull of a trigger
simple to do
not hard to figure.
Set your sights
and out flies the lead
before the bang reaches you
you're face down and dead.

And here I am in Army green
acting big, bad, and mean
but inside I'm still the same
to me this all is just a game.

"Fix bayonets," is the order heard,

sweat runs down your brow
you dare not say a word.
In the kill zone
you stab and slash
crimson flies from a nasty gash.
Today guts spill
and you don't ask why.
Is this your day
to live or die?

But here I am in Army Green
acting big, bad, and mean
but inside
am I still the same?
To me this all
was just a game.

This is the game of life
a deadly game of take or lose your life.

But someday this could be real
and then you won't know how you'll feel.
Can you set your sights
and easily squeeze?
Can you crush a man
down to his knees?
Oh, dear God,
don't test us, please.

Prelude to Peace and Whore-money

Written in 1997, I look at this poem and seeing where we're at in 2020, some things just never change. This was a call to the people to take a look at what was going on in a global view.

Peace and Whore-money

Gas prices are rising
most of the Muslim countries are despising
and we're still compromising.

Now if we are the caretakers of the world
as we think.
Don't you believe we're due?
No questions.
No stink.

How much of the Earth owes us something?

How many lives do we have to save
or how many more
should we put in a grave?

Where are the boundaries
between wrong and right?
Is this all about money
or is there still harmony in sight?
If money has become our main objective
is peace now an alternative elective?

Prelude to Colorblind?

Coming from a predominately white background, I was proud to be one of the newer generations to not see color as much as our predecessors did. In the Army I had plenty of other-than-white friends and one of my favorite saying was "We are all green here and we all bleed red." Once submersed in the underworld, I came to appreciate other colors and did so quickly. Prejudice I never quite got.

Colorblind?

White
black
yellow
red.
What's it matter after all is said?

I hate you because of the color of your skin
come on, fools,
you just can't win.

Uzi sprays its deadly fire
indiscrete to who goes higher.

KKK kills another
leaves six children
and a lonely mother.

Now, my friends,
don't you see
the question of color
is not for you or me?

Let's talk about racism.
Let's talk about you and I.
Let's talk about the news
and the various ways we die.
In the long run
let's talk about why.

Prelude to The Treasure Hunter, Decision Time, and The Pugilist

The Treasure Hunter was written in 2001, in jail, to Amy Booth of Ft. Collins, Colorado. Amy and I had been together from 1995-1998. A librarian scholarly type, she was the exact opposite of me, as this was the high point of my organized crime days. I kept Amy blind to the true goings-on, but she did have an inkling about what I did. An emotionless period of my life, I wasn't capable of giving her what she needed and deserved. Turning myself into the law in 2000 and trying to straighten out my life, I thought perhaps I could rekindle things and give her what she was due. One letter was written from jail but was never answered.

Decision Time and The Pugilist written at the same period were obviously written at the crossroads where I desperately wanted to change.

The Treasure Hunter

I've lost the greatest treasure
that I have ever found
be it not gold or diamonds
or even pearls in an endless mound.

I've traveled the entire world
seeking something to compare
a desperate time of searching
for that, that was so rare.

I've gone so far
as to climb the highest mountain
and dive the deepest sea
trying to regain that glorious treasure
that now seems to elude me.

I got myself a starship
to travel endless space
but nothing could compare to my loss
much to my disgrace.

I sharpened up the finest sword
and the greatest dragon
I did slay.
The jewels were most abundant
but my longing
was not quenched this day.

I've traced my heart's desire
and now know where it lies
the greatest of all treasures
was deep within your eyes.

Decision Time

Concrete walls
and stainless steel
sitting in this jail cell
waiting for a judge's appeal.

By society's laws
I guess I've done wrong.
obviously so
singing this chain gang song.

Where did I drift
from the righteous path?
Have I gone far enough
to feel God's wrath?

What can possibly
set my ways right?
Of Heaven and Hell
who's winning this fight?

They call for chow
we all get in line
don't look right or left
forward is fine.

Shovel your slop
as fast as you can
speak not a word
is your best plan.

The lights go out
and it's a good time to pray
to ask for forgiveness
and to make it one more day.

And as you look
to Heaven above
do you keep wondering who's winning
hatred or love?

Finally the day comes
and they'll set you free
but now the question of who's winning
is up to you and me.

One road goes left
the other right
one stinks of sulfur
the other feels of might.

Decision time
choose your fate
your life lies ahead
love or hate?

The Pugilist
(or in Layman's Terms, The Boxer)

Fireman
Doctor
Indian chief
maybe an Astronaut
or the President
to my parents' relief.

But sometimes it doesn't work out
the greatest fight of your life
the narcotic, booze bout
and by round number three
I was knocked the "F" out.

Round Number One
I stood confident and tall
no way in this life
would this boy take a fall.

On top of the world
ahead of the pack
beer, pot combination
and I was flat on my back.

Not one to stay down
I popped back to my feet
whisky, coke jab
and I was out in the street.

Now in
Round Number Two
I had a new goal
using in moderation
would save my soul.

Came out of my corner
ended up in a bar
uppercut on the chin
and I was driving a car.

I hooked to the left
took one on the nose,

"Only had two beers, Occifer,"

you know how the story goes.

So it's
Round Number Three
you already know the end
came out of my corner
then thought I'd pretend.

Jab, jab, duck, hook
a pugilist I did look
I knew for certain
I'd fool 'em all by the book.

Heroin haymaker to the head
vodka shot to the liver
I started to feel weak
and my legs began to quiver.

I finally gave out
and took a big fall
and that's how I ended
behind this jailhouse wall.

A comeback is in the making
my career is not over
I'll step back in the ring
and give him a good once-over.

There'll be one big difference
this next opening round
for once in my life
sobriety's found.

Prelude to Lucky Cop Gets Nine-to-Five Job

This was written post-Columbine shooting, a very different style from my usual "grown-up Dr. Seuss" stanzas. It's a look at the future that was to quickly approach. My Uncle Vern, a big fan of my poetry, read half and said, "This is garbage!" I asked him to at least finish it and by the end he had changed his opinion. I get a different perspective from all that read this, good and bad.

Lucky Cop Gets Nine-to-Five Job

The gargantuan man in blue
stood especially attentive
this beautiful October morning
a slight chill
in the autumn breeze.

This always made them
restless.

He was prepared
this well-trained
protector of the peace.

Senses
trouble
before he even awakes.
Today
might be the day.

Slight perspiration
on his brow.
Holster the large caliber
in case.
Safe side.

Metal detector duty.
One by one
issued through.

Sinister cherub faces.

Nothing.
Nothing.
Nothing.

Electronic beep
screams danger

Hairs rise instantly
on instantly chilled neck.
Hand finds gun
Handle
as quickly as possible.
Is this it?
Am I ready?

"You,
step to the side."

Sinister cherub faces.

Metal scanner
wails trouble.
Upper-right side
inside jacket pocket.

Tension.
Slowly remove.
Easy now.

Forgotten coins.
Instant relief.
Deep breath.

"Move on."

Sweat bead trickles
down face.

He hates first period
recess even more
and their sinister cherub faces.

Prelude to Gaea

Gaea is a Greek goddess caring for Earth and the belief that the Earth is a living, breathing organism. The human race possibly being a parasitic pest. This was written after the hurricane and the tsunami devastation of 2004.

Gaea

The tiniest of organisms
in the great measurement of things
had tolerated the parasites
for the briefest of moments
in the idea of time.

But now the irritant
could be ignored
no longer
and the living mass shuddered
as canines will sometimes do
freeing themselves of annoying fleas.

Peace was its reward
and the Earth rested
cleansed and healthy.

Prelude to Walls and Mistimed Love

This was written in 2008 after marriage counseling. My emotional blockade of eighteen years had finally been broken through. A complete reversal in our relationship occurred where I now needed and craved affection and Becca had become remote and cold. These were my two final pleas.

Walls

I did you wrong
for so long.
A selfish man
wrapped up in
his own inner plan.

An emotionless hole
leaving you
my Muse
endlessly pursuing
true love as your goal.

And though you thought
what you found
was your heart's desire
it soon became clear
that this man
had long ago
lost his fire.

And the passionate
fun-filled being
that I married
and grew to know
is maybe long lost
a longing for love in tow.

And this amazing
beautiful being
that shined so bright
looked at me heartbroken
as I put the last brick in place
to complete the wall
and extinguish her light.

And then sometimes
as fate will do
a sudden spark ignited
and lit anew
those long-dead feelings
and passions so true
and the man opened his eyes
and immediately knew.

He broke from his prison
the cold walls tumbling down
and looked for his Muse
but she was nowhere
to be found.

Like a new naked soul
he bared his heart
begging and pleading
for a fresh new start.

But of course
the pleas went unheard
for the Muse's walls
long ago complete
had been finished
with a dark mortar
of bitter resentment concrete.

Screaming now
from the depths of his soul
hammering and chipping
to get to his goal.

His mind balanced
on the brink of madness
and the thoughts of what he'd done
surrounded his heart
with the ultimate sadness.

The Muse within
could hear his calls
but the most unfortunate thing had happened
she had begun to like her walls.

That wonderful spirit
so open and free
now locked away
could not be harmed
by the likes of me

His newfound yearning for love
had become a disease
the broken
tired man
fell to his knees.

Closing his eyes
he leaned up against the wall
the torn man waits
in hopes
someday
it still might fall.

The wall stands steady
hard and cold
crumbling not
for the heartache I've told.

But what this man
did not know
is that his Muse
had built an escape passage
long ago
and at any point
she could set herself free
so, beaten man,
hang in there
be patient
you'll just have to wait
and see.

Mistimed Love

It pains me to say
that I love you more
each and every day.

Six years have flown by
and that lust that I lacked
for reasons untold
are now at full force
double fold.

Every day you amaze me more.
I want to move forward
and see what's in store.
It's only you
that I adore.

I look at you with a combination
of love and lust.
You've broken down my walls
and have my unabated trust.

Yet the question of pain
does still remain.

How is it possible
to have in your midst
your heart's desire
and due to mistiming
she no longer feels that fire?

Will your heart ever soften
and know this is true?
Only one person knows this answer
and that person is you.

I'll beg and I'll plead.
Just another chance
is all that I need.

It's been several lifetimes
since emotions were involved
but that's what you brought out of me
as our love has evolved
just one more chance
and my pain could be solved

Prelude to The Lost and Found and Day of No Regrets Long Gone

These were both done during my first stay in the psych ward just prior to the beginning of A "Bird's" Journey. The Lost and Found was written as a release from the insanity plaguing me. It is the story of how I got there and once there, my seeing the vets and the help they needed.

Days of No Regrets Long Gone was also written as a healing, therapeutic poem at this time. A poem of realization. A slightly different style, as I tried to attach everything to the rhyme of "-un."

The Lost and Found

Madness settled in...

a gun
a bullet
a bottle of booze
struggling to pull the trigger
looking forward to the eternal snooze.

Called the soon-to-be ex,

"Come and meet me here,
I got a plan
I got a gun,"

I choked out through a tear.

The girl I love so dearly
this is where the madness rises
she doesn't love me in return
and there are no compromises.

Missed my turn to meet her
a blessing in disguise
still want to pull the trigger
and let my spirit rise.

Cops rolling up the next street
I know full well
this is not their beat.
A dodge
a twist
and I retreat.

Next turn I take is highway bound
North to die
South to be found
VA hospital
how profound.

> "Find a doctor
> find a nurse
> gun's in my car
> love's my curse."

Psychiatric ward is calling
government-funded drugs
have them all falling.
Depression they say is my ill
take this little happy pill.
If that's not enough
you can have your fill.

I've met the vets
on the second floor
good guys all
that's for sure
can tell my stay
will not be a bore.

Some of their minds are blown.
Others hear gunfire
and see death being sown.
Some are just so sad
you can hear it
in their tone.
While others still can't stop their buddies
from hitting the tripwire
and watching their bodies
being thrown.

Some hospitals have thrown them away
like bread so stale
or fruit so rotten
but these are your vets
let them not be forgotten.

As for me
the heart will heal
look after your vets
this is my final appeal.

Days of No Regrets Long Gone

Regrets...

I used to say that I had none.
Now with the end of my marriage
I have a proverbial ton.
Love's been lost
seemingly not again ever to be re-won.
What was to be a beautiful thing
got twisted up
and certainly has not ended up any fun.
Having now to look into the past
and the damage that was done.
I know the hurt
I feel the pain

                    "Don't look at me like that, son."

Even on my worst enemy
I'd wish this on no one.
The pressure continues to build up
like a supernova exploding sun.

Would I be a bigger man to go on
or end it with a gun?
As usual I hear Death calling
and instead of standing and facing it
all I do is run.
I guess for now
I'll just keep going
and end this little pun.

Prelude to The Swim and
The Man Who Loves and Misses You

The Swim was written just prior to finding myself unable to find a ride to the beach. I found myself next standing on the road's edge gauging vehicle speeds and whether or not they were fast enough to get the job done. This poem originally ended after the sixth stanza as a goodbye letter. The second part was added on in my second stay at the psych ward by the suggestion of a friend. She found it simply too sad to leave it as it was and I agreed with her.

The Man Who Loves and Misses You was also written at this time as an apology to my children and again coming to terms with the fact that my marriage was over.

The Swim

A trip to the ocean
to ease the emotion
no need for lotion
as this is my goodbye devotion.

My love for my wife
it runs so deep
I miss her so much
as I swim out to sleep.

The moon glistens off the sea
as I swim out far to be free.
God, is this a sin?
I guess we'll wait and see.

And now I dive
into the deep
I pray the Lord
my soul to keep
and if I should drown
below the ocean wake
I pray the Lord
my soul to take.

My children
I'm so sorry
know I'll be watching from somewhere
and know that Daddy loves you
and that he really did care.

And as selfish as this may be
know that Mommy
will make you a better man
a better man than me
listen
be good, kids
I'll be checking in to see.
And the me
as a man
swims out into the sea
as far as the soul can
to finally be set free.

And now I dive
into the deep
I pray the Lord
my soul to keep
and if I should drown
below the ocean wake
I pray the Lord
my soul to take.

But waking in a cold sweat
this is just a dream
hasn't happened yet.

I wish somebody had warned me
that love was going to be so hard
hopefully someday
I'll once again be able to let down my guard.

I'll still struggle
and hold on to hope
reality is
it'll be a rocky slope.

Though God may test us
up this steep hill
He'll never give us enough
to break our will.

And march you may
with a broken sandal
He'll never give you more
than He knows that you can handle.

Even though sometimes
you may think all is lost
just never give up
at all cost.

So just hang in there
and ignore the dream
it's never as bad
as it may seem.

And now I lay me
down to sleep
I pray the Lord
my soul to keep
and if I should die
before I wake
I pray the Lord
my soul to take.

The Man Who Loves and Misses You

My little ones keep asking,

        "Why, Daddy, aren't you coming home?"

All I know to tell them is that,

        "Mommy wants to be alone."

But this would be a lie, I think,
as Mommy's still looking for a man
I just can't tell my sons
I'm no longer in the plan.

But Daddy still loves Mommy
so very, very much
I promise to try to be there
on holidays and such.

But Mommy's moving on
with her new, happy life
and Daddy's heart is broken
still wanting her to be his wife.

But daddies should be stronger
I know that this is true
my children, I'm so sorry
but I had many an issue.

I'm trying to put the pieces
back together once again
but Daddy not only lost his wife
but also his best friend.

Daughter, know I love you
so very, very much
I promise to try to be there
on holidays and such.

But Mommy's moving on
going out and having fun
and Daddy's mind has sickened
thinking that Mommy and Daddy
should still be one.

But husbands should be stronger
I know that this is true
my wife, I'm just so sorry
as my heart was torn in two.

And although I've lost it all
kids
house
job
and mind
seemingly included
never hold anything against Mommy.
The strongest of men
I was not
as I've already eluded.

Sons, know that I still love you
so very, very much
I promise to try to be there
on holidays and such.

And though Daddy misses Mommy
his life
his love
his wife
perhaps it's time for Daddy
to step out
into his all-new life.

My children, I am so sorry
for all of us
this will be rough.
Know that Daddy still loves all of you
through good times
and even tough.

And though Daddy may not be there
as much as I would hope
we'll all just have to hang in there
and learn how we can cope.

I want you all to know
I love you
daughter
sons
and wife included.
This is my apology
from the heart
and on that
it is concluded.

Prelude to Mission Accomplished

Mission Accomplished was commissioned for a vet in the psych ward. He was a fan of my poetry and asked me to write something that would inspire his dreams and the dreams of others also. It was a blessing in disguise, as my more recent poetry had been dark and brooding. Mission Accomplished not only inspired him and other vets but myself also.

Mission Accomplished

With nothing ventured
there's nothing gained.
Grab ahold of your dreams
It's all that may remain.

Put forth the effort
and you can do it all.
Without an attempt
you'll always fall.

The great fault
of many a man
is not holding true
to his own inner plan.

Grip tight to your dreams
and venture forth.
It's the only way
to find your true self-worth.

Just know that always
it may not go as planned.
Don't let your pride
keep you
from accepting a helping hand.

And the charge for my tuition?
Nothing.
Just live by your goal
and you'll always see fruition.

So as you can see
this advice is free.
It's up to you to take the first step
a leap of faith is the key.

Charge forth as a warrior
with this brand-new shield.
And to any adversity
let your inner strength never yield.

Live your life
with your goals achieved
even though nobody else
may have believed.

And at this point
you can look upon high
feeling emptiness no longer
and having to ask the question why.

And that pride that you feel and fills your heart
is the beginning of your new life
and a fresh, new start.

Let's just always remember
to look up in the sky
constantly give thanks
and never again ask why.

Prelude to Mother "Bird"

Mother "Bird" was written in my fourth stay in a drug and alcohol program. My poor mother had been asking for a poem for twenty years, finally she got what she was asking for. I love you, Mom, remember, sometimes it takes a lifetime.

Mother Bird

The "Bird" mother
well, she's like no other.
Always there on the spot
making sure things are all right
needed or not.

And now as autumn settles in
she can take a look back
to see where she's been.

All her baby birds
now have their own nests.
Most with fledglings of their own
now putting them to the test.
The Mother Bird
had done her best.

But her journey
wasn't so easy with this one Baby "Bird."
He always took the wrong path
and flew places that were absurd.

But she was there
to try and guide him right.
It left Mother Bird nervous
and always uptight
just wishing someday
Baby "Bird" would get it right.

Well, he flew many places
both light and dark
and at many times
his future looked stark.

But Mother Bird was there
to love and to care
but at times it seemed
just too much to bear.

Then one day an acorn
fell from an ancient tree
and Baby "Bird" eating poison berries
simply did not see.

It tumbled down
hitting Baby "Bird" in the head
and when he came to
this is what he said,

> "Mother Bird, in your wisdom
> many times you were right.
> Though try as you may
> you couldn't pick my flight.
> I appreciate you always being there
> morning
> noon
> and night.
> But now I'm trying a new flight path
> and my future is starting to seem bright.
> It took a major hit on the head
> but I finally see the light."

So worry no longer
it'll do you no good
trust in Baby "Bird" to make the choices
he knows that he should.

And so for Mother Bird and Baby "Bird"
the best of times are yet to be.
Mother Bird, sit back
watch and enjoy the autumn.
Fret not.
Relax.
Just wait and you'll see.

Prelude to I've Been...

This was written as a reminder that we should never forget where we've come from, good and bad.

I've Been...

I've been a fighter
and a fucker
and a fool.

I've been the smartest kid
in class
and kicked out of school.

I've been a poet and a soldier
and a sugar mama's toy.
Baby, I'm a lover
and a leaver.
Your mother's favorite boy.
But I always kept you up to date on the score
so don't start acting coy.

I grew up on a farm
and ran drugs from Mexico.
I've been a scholar and a gangster
a pimp and a hoe.

I've been a star athlete
and a beach bum
in riches and rags.
On my worst days down and out
I even rolled fags.

I've been a haole and a prep
and I've worn cowboy boots.
I'm a Celtic warrior
if you track down my roots.

I've been a loony in a bin
and a committer of sin.
Some see me as a pillar of society
but they don't know where I've been.

I've been a junky and a drunk
and debated religion with a monk.
I've been an ugly man
and considered a hunk.

I've been a punk and a rocker
and a lover of Beethoven.
Life is full of choices
and it's intricately woven.

I've been a speaker of truths
and a teller of lies.
I've saved a man's life
and turned my head when someone dies.

I've walked with thousands in my pocket
and not had a penny to my name.
But wherever I came to
it was always all the same.

I've been homeless
and I've lived in high society.
I've been caged like an animal
and I've been truly free.

I've been a husband and a father
and a triggerman.
Look around at your neighbors
do you know who I am?

Tomorrow I could lose or I could win
but at least I can say that I've been.